Utah

Facts and Symbols

by Kathy Feeney

Consultant:
Ken Kraus
Media Relations Manager
Utah Travel Council

Hilltop Books

an imprint of Capstone Press
Mankato, Minnesota

Hilltop Books are published by Capstone Press
151 Good Counsel Drive, P.O. Box 669, Mankato, Minnesota 56002
http://www.capstone-press.com

Library of Congress Cataloging-in-Publication Data
Feeney, Kathy, 1954–
    Utah facts and symbols/by Kathy Feeney
    p. cm.—(The states and their symbols)
    Includes bibliographical references (p. 23) and index.
    Summary: Presents information about the state of Utah, its nickname, motto,
and emblems.
    ISBN 0-7368-0526-5
    1. Emblems, State—Utah—Juvenile literature. [1. Emblems, State—Utah.
2. Utah.] I. Title. II. Series.

CR203.U8 F44 2000
979.2—dc21   99-053457

Editorial Credits
Karen L. Daas, editor; Linda Clavel, production designer and illustrator;
    Kimberly Danger, photo researcher

Photo Credits
Christian Heeb/Jon Gnass Photo Images, 6
James P. Rowan, 16, 22 (top)
Jeff March Nature Photography, 14, 20
Kent and Donna Dannen, 22 (middle)
One Mile Up, Inc., 8, 10 (inset)
Rob and Ann Simpson, 12
Robert McCaw, 18
Root Resources/John Kohout, cover; James Blank, 10
Visuals Unlimited/Ken Martin, 22 (bottom)

2 3 4 5 6 05 04 03 02

Table of Contents

Fast Facts

Capital: Salt Lake City is the capital of Utah.

Largest City: Salt Lake City also is the largest city in Utah. More than 172,575 people live in Salt Lake City.

Size: Utah covers 84,990 square miles (220,124 square kilometers). It is the 11th largest state.

Location: Utah is in the western United States.

Population: 2,099,758 people live in Utah (U.S. Census Bureau, 1998 estimate).

Statehood: On January 4, 1896, Utah became the 45th state to join the union.

Natural Resources: Utah's natural resources include granite, gold, silver, copper, natural gas, salt, and uranium.

Manufactured Goods: Companies in Utah make food, chemicals, computer parts, and spacecraft parts.

Crops: Farmers in Utah grow barley, hay, potatoes, onions, apricots, and cherries. They raise cows and sheep.

State Name and Nickname

Early European explorers named Utah after the Utes. This Native American group lived high in the mountains of Utah. "Ute" means "high place."

Utah's nickname is the Beehive State. This nickname came from the word "deseret," which means "honey bee." The first Mormon settlers called Utah "The Provisional State of Deseret." Mormons are members of the Church of Jesus Christ of Latter-day Saints. Many Mormons settled in Utah. Today, about 70 percent of Utahns are Mormon.

The Salt Lake State is another nickname for Utah. The Great Salt Lake is in northern Utah. It is the largest salt lake in North America. The Great Salt Lake also is the largest natural lake west of the Mississippi River.

Utah is known as the "State of Adventure." The state's mountains and sand dunes attract many visitors.

The Great Salt Lake is about four times more salty than any of the world's oceans.

THE GREAT SEAL OF THE STATE OF UTAH

INDUSTRY

1847

1896

State Seal and Motto

Utah's government adopted its state seal in 1896. The seal represents Utah's government. It also makes state government papers official.

Many symbols appear on Utah's state seal. An American bald eagle stands for protection during peace and war. A beehive represents hard work. Sego lilies are on both sides of the beehive. These flowers stand for peace. Two U.S. flags appear on the seal. The flags show that Utah is part of the United States.

Two dates appear on the seal. The date 1847 is in the center. Mormons first settled in what is now Utah in 1847. Utah became a state in 1896. This year appears at the bottom of the seal.

Utah's motto appears on the state seal. Government officials adopted "Industry" as the state motto in 1959. Business and hard work are important to Utahns.

Six small arrows appear on the shield in the center of the seal. They represent protection for Utah during times of war.

State Capitol and Flag

Salt Lake City is the capital of Utah. Utah's capitol building is in Salt Lake City. Government officials meet there to make the state's laws.

Richard K. A. Kletting designed Utah's capitol. Workers built the capitol on a hill in Salt Lake City. They completed the capitol in 1915.

Workers used Utah granite and Georgia marble to build Utah's capitol. Tall pillars line the front of the capitol. Pillars also support a dome ceiling. The dome ceiling is 165 feet (50 meters) above the floor. Inside, a painting of seagulls appears on the ceiling. The seagull is Utah's state bird. Stone lions sit at the entrance of the capitol.

Utah has had two state flags. The first state flag was adopted in 1896. The current state flag was adopted in 1913. This flag has a blue background. Utah's state seal appears on the center of the flag.

Utah's current state flag originally flew over the battleship _Utah_.

State Bird

The seagull became Utah's state bird in 1955. People remembered a time that seagulls helped the state's farmers. In 1848, locusts attacked crops in Utah. Locusts are grasshoppers that eat crops. Farmers thought their families would starve. But seagulls ate the locusts and saved many farmers' crops.

Adult seagulls have white and light gray feathers. Their legs are pale green. Their bills are red. Seagulls may have red rings around their eyes.

Seagulls live near large bodies of water. They eat small animals, insects, and even garbage. Seagulls have waterproof feathers. Seagulls' webbed feet make them excellent swimmers. Their long wingspan makes them strong, graceful flyers.

A bronze monument of a seagull stands in Salt Lake City. Mahonri Young created the monument to honor the seagull for saving early farmers' crops. It was dedicated in 1913.

Many seagulls swim in Utah's Great Salt Lake.

State Tree

The blue spruce became Utah's official state tree in 1933. These trees grow in Utah's mountain forests. Many Utahns plant blue spruce trees in their yards. Blue spruce trees also are called Colorado blue spruce or silver spruce.

The blue spruce is a large tree. A blue spruce can grow to be 200 feet (61 meters) tall. These trees sometimes live more than 600 years.

Blue spruce trees are evergreens. Evergreen trees have leaves all year. Blue spruce leaves are short, sharp needles. These needles live for about 10 years. New needles then grow to replace old needles. A thick wax coats blue spruce needles. This wax gives blue spruce trees their silver-blue color.

Some Utah companies use wood from blue spruce trees to make paper. Companies also sell these trees for Christmas trees.

Light brown cones grow on blue spruce trees. The cones hold seeds.

State Flower

The sego lily became Utah's official state flower in 1911. Utah's schoolchildren chose the sego lily. The sego lily was important to Utah's Native Americans and Mormon settlers. They used the sego lily for food.

Sego lilies are wildflowers. They grow throughout Utah and the western United States. Sego lilies bloom in midsummer. They have thin green stems. Sego lilies have white, tulip-shaped blossoms. Each blossom has a yellow base with purple markings.

Native Americans taught Utah's early settlers about sego lilies. Native Americans showed settlers how to uproot sego lilies. They taught settlers how to grind and prepare sego lily bulbs as food. These bulbs taste sweet. Early settlers ate sego lily bulbs when their crops were destroyed or did not grow.

To Utahns, sego lilies are a sign of peace.

State Animal

Utah's government adopted the Rocky Mountain elk as the official state animal in 1971. Rocky Mountain elk once roamed Utah's mountains. Early settlers hunted the animal for food and leather. Today, many Rocky Mountain elk live in national parks and wildlife refuges.

Rocky Mountain elk are gray-brown. They have a short, stubby tail. Adult elk grow to about 5 feet (1.5 meters) tall and almost 8 feet (2.4 meters) long. They eat grass.

Female elk are called cows. They usually weigh about 500 pounds (227 kilograms). Male elk are called bulls. They usually weigh about 700 pounds (318 kilograms). A bull elk's antlers can grow to more than 5 feet (1.5 meters) across.

Female Rocky Mountain elk give birth to one calf each year. Calves are born in late spring or early summer.

Rocky Mountain elk belong to the deer family. They are related to moose and caribou.

More State Symbols

State Centennial Star: In 1996, Utah chose the star Dubhe as the state centennial star. Dubhe is a star in the Big Dipper constellation. This group of stars looks like a soup ladle.

State Cooking Pot: The Dutch oven was named the state cooking pot in 1997. This pot has three legs and a flat top. Early settlers cooked fruit cobblers and stews in the pot. Utahns still use Dutch ovens.

State Fossil: A dinosaur called Allosaurus became Utah's state fossil in 1988. Scientists have found many Allosaurus bones in Utah.

State Grass: Indian ricegrass was named Utah's state grass in 1990. Utah's Native Americans used this grass for food. They ground the grass seeds into flour to make bread.

State Insect: The honey bee became the state insect in 1983. The honey bee is important in Mormon history.

Fifth-grade students in Utah chose the honey bee as the state insect.

Places to Visit

Bryce Canyon National Park

Bryce Canyon National Park is near the town of Tropic. Bryce Canyon became a national park in 1928. Millions of years of erosion created the great gorge called Bryce Canyon. Visitors tour the park on foot or on horseback. Visitors enjoy the beautiful landscape and wildlife of the park.

Dinosaur National Monument

Dinosaur National Monument is in northeastern Utah. Scientists found a large number of dinosaur bones near the monument. The site became a national monument in 1915. Visitors can see dinosaur bones preserved in the monument's sandstone wall.

Great Salt Lake

The Great Salt Lake is west of Salt Lake City. The Great Salt Lake is the largest salt lake in North America. Visitors stroll along the beaches of the Great Salt Lake. Some visitors go boating on the lake. Visitors also swim in the lake's salty water.

Words to Know

antlers (ANT-lurs)—bony structures on a male elk's head
canyon (KAN-yuhn)—a long, deep valley
constellation (kon-stuh-LAY-shuhn)—a group of stars that forms a shape
erosion (ih-ROH-zhuhn)—the gradual wearing away of a substance by water or wind
evergreen (EV-ur-green)—a tree that has leaves all year
fossil (FOSS-uhl)—the remains of an animal or a plant that have been preserved in rock
locust (LOH-kust)—a type of grasshopper that destroys and eats crops
Mormon (MOR-muhn)—a member of the Church of Jesus Christ of Latter-day Saints

Read More

Fradin, Dennis B. *Utah.* From Sea to Shining Sea. Chicago: Children's Press, 1997.

Kummer, Patricia K. *Utah.* One Nation. Mankato, Minn.: Capstone High/Low Books, 1998.

Thompson, Kathleen. *Utah.* Portrait of America. Austin, Texas: Raintree Steck-Vaughn, 1996.

Useful Addresses

Salt Lake Convention and Visitors Bureau
90 South West Temple
Salt Lake City, UT 84101

Utah Travel Council
Council Hall/Capitol Hill
Salt Lake City, UT 84114

Internet Sites

State of Utah
http://www.state.ut.us/education/kidspage.html
Utah State Historical Society
http://history.utah.org/KKid_s/kkidspage.html
Utah State Symbols
http://www.state.ut.us/about/symbols.html
Utah Travel Council
http://www.utah.com

Index